LEARNING TO DREAM

WITH YOUR EYES OPEN

A SURVIVAL GUIDE FOR INNER CITY YOUTH

Melanie D. Geddes

Learning Series Press

Florida

ISBN: 0-9769701-0-4

Library of Congress Control Number: 2005904511

First Printing 2005
McNaughton & Gunn, Inc.
Printed in the United States of America

Book Design by John Carman/Avenue Design

Learning Series Press
P.O. Box 590812
Fort Lauderdale, FL 33359
Email us at: info@learningtodream.com
Website: www.learningtodream.com

In loving memory of my brother,

Curtis Wilkes

LEARNING TO DREAM

WITH YOUR EYES OPEN

Contents

What "They" Said About Me...

They said I had a better chance of being incarcerated
than being educated.

They said I was more likely to drop out or cop out.

They said I'd have children when I was a kid myself,
And the kids would have to be cared for by somebody else.

They said my body would be plagued
by poor and failing health.

They laughed at the prospect of me accumulating wealth.

They said I'd never marry and never live in a house.

They wrote me off as "a good for nothing louse".

Because I was born into poverty,
they said that's where I'd remain.

They determined that before adulthood
I'd either kill or I'd be slain.

They said I'd never move out of the projects...
and if I did, it would be with Section 8.

They said that eventually, I'd be sorry,
but by then, it would be too late.

They said I'd spend all my money on frivolous things;
like fancy cars, diamonds, and two-finger rings.

They said that saving and investing
was beyond my comprehension.

They never even considered I could one day earn a pension.

They said that I was lazy and didn't really want to work.

They said I'd rather wait on the government "perks".

They said that I'd sell drugs and if not, I'd be addicted.

They said I'd commit a crime and at some point,
I'd get convicted.

They said I was more likely to get HIV than an MPA.

But I proved you wrong, didn't I "They"?

— Melanie Geddes

ACKNOWLEDGEMENTS

To my mother who always made me believe that I had something special to offer the world, I love you. To my sister Joyce, who believes in me more than I believe in myself, I love you girl! To my husband Sean, who has been telling me to write for years, thank you for believing in me and supporting me before there was a light in the tunnel. I love you. To my sons, Shaun and Shane, and my nephew, Jarell, don't ever stop dreaming. Don't ever stop believing. I love you guys! To my brothers, Antoine, Barkee, and Edward, keep doing the right thing…even when no one is watching. I love you guys. To Aunt Rose, Aunt Gloria and my cousin Danielle, thanks so much for providing a helping hand since day one. I remember, and I am extremely grateful. To Ms. Ruth, Ms. Osie, Ms. Shirley and Ms. Carmen, thank you for treating me as if I were your own daughter. To my friends, thank you for helping me to understand the true meaning of friendship and for always being willing to help. A special thanks to my "sistahs", Rasheem, Beshon, Camilla, and Kiva, for always keepin' it real and for sticking with me through all of my growing pains.

My sincere appreciation goes to my brother-in-law Everton, and to my friends Tina, Howard, Rosezener, and Anita for your support on this project. Your words of encouragement, advice and assistance with the development of the book mean more to me than you will ever know. I want to thank JoAnn Woodside, of Comma Consultants, for copyediting my work, John Carman of Avenue Design for designing the book cover and interior layout, and Shafqat Ali for creating such an awesome website. There are not enough words for me to explain how much I appreciate the late hours you spent working on the site. Thanks a million! To Gary Manning and David Reid who offered help at pivotal times in my life, thank you. Last but not least, I want to thank all of the people who have helped me to become the woman I am today. I extend my sincerest gratitude to all of my relatives, friends, teachers, professors, and supervisors who challenged me to give more when I thought that I had nothing left to give.

There is more in us than we know. If we can be made to see it, perhaps, for the rest of our lives, we will be unwilling to settle for less.

— Kurt Hahn

Introduction

Have you ever been inspired by something great that someone else did? Have you ever gotten so fired up about doing something extraordinary and then talked yourself out of it? Do you look around at your circumstances and adjust your goals? Do you tell yourself that it would be easier to try something else or that you are more likely to be successful if you aim for the sure target?

Well, it's no surprise that most people never figure out what their true purposes are and, admittedly, are not completely happy about the paths that their lives have taken. I believe it's because it is easier to talk yourself *out* of success than to talk yourself *into* it.

Let me be the first to say that your circumstances can impact your starting point, but they don't necessarily determine your ending point. I am a firm believer that we can achieve whatever we pursue with passion, drive, dedication, resilience and unrelenting persistence.

Yes, there are some people who are born into inheritance, and success for them may seem inevitable. Yes, there are those who get "lucky" and stumble into the opportunity of a lifetime. But most of us who live in the real world have never met anybody who didn't have to struggle to achieve his or her triumphs.

I invite you to clear your mind of self-doubt and negativity and travel with me on a journey to self-confidence—a place where "can't" does not exist, "can" has a temporary lease, and "am", "will" and "did" live together harmoniously. Discover the place within where all things are possible.

During the course of this journey it is my hope that you will come to realize that you already possess many of the attributes necessary for success. I hope you will come to realize that everything you don't already have is within your reach.

Each chapter will end with a "Lesson Learned" activity. The purpose of these activities is to help you find personal meaning in each chapter and to encourage you to reflect on your role in improving your situation.

It is my hope you will decide for yourself that making your dreams a reality is an important priority. It is my hope you will be inspired to set and achieve your goals.

I hope you will realize that you are not alone, and that others have traveled the same journey, run the same race, and fought the same fight. I am one of them.

Although I cannot travel the road beside you or run the race with you, I am here for you. No, I am not at the same place as you are on the journey, but I was there before. This book is my way of leaving pebbles in the dirt to help you find your way.

I may not be in the race, but I am on the side-lines. I am the one handing you the cup of water to help you continue on as you race towards the finish line. I won't be in the ring to help you fight your way through the tough times, but I will be in your corner.

I care about you, I believe in you, and I am counting on you to make it.

I advise you to say that your dream is possible and then overcome all inconveniences, ignore all the hassles and take a running leap through the hoop even if it is in flames.

— **Les Brown**

CHAPTER 1

WHY DREAM?

"*Dr.* *Phil don't know nothin' 'bout my life. He can't tell me nothin'. All those talk shows and books out there to help you solve your problems and fix your life, but none of the people giving that advice could live a day in my world. I live in the Inner City. Drugs, sex, violence, and poverty surround me. That's my reality. That's my problem. I don't have a role model. I'm traveling without a map. I'm figuring this thing out as I go along. You can't even begin to understand the complexities of everyday living in "the hood". My surroundings are depressing. My community is deteriorating. The hallways in my building reek of urine. The floors are dirty and littered with trash. The lights are dim...if there is any light at all. There's always someone loitering in the lobby selling or smoking some illegal drug. This is what greets me every day as I exit my apartment to go to school. When I return home from school, nothing has changed. Darkness or nightfall only adds more drama. On any given night I may have to get out of my bed and lie flat on the floor because of a shoot-out occurring beneath my window. If I'm lucky, the only noise I will hear is a neighbor arguing or fighting...or tunes blasting out of the speakers of somebody's boom box. I can deal with that. I'm used to it.*

My family is poor. We struggle on a daily basis to make ends meet. Sometimes we don't even have a decent meal to eat. I bet the Doc and his family eat a lavish meal every night. Trust me, I'm not playa hatin'. I just don't want nobody tryin' to paint me a rosy picture and telling me they can help me fix my life if I tune into their show or buy their book when they don't know nothin' about where I come from. It really bothers me when these people try to relate their situation to mine. From what I see, their lives are a cakewalk. I'm just trying to survive in a world where there ain't no "Toy's-R-Us Kids". You gotta grow up quick. You don't have a choice. Situations and circumstances are rough. So, while some kids my age are playin' dodge ball with their friends, me and my friends are dodgin' bullets. Me and my friends are afraid to dream because reality keeps us wide-awake."

Although the above is written fictitiously, as a product of the Inner City I know that many inner city youth have the exact same feelings because they are subjected to a similar lifestyle. They feel that their situation is hopeless and give up on success without ever really taking the steps to be successful. They have learned to live day-by-day.

Life in "the hood" is sometimes so overwhelming that people tend to ignore the true state of confusion and despair associated with it. People from the Inner City often adapt to their environment so well that they don't even see a problem with their daily surroundings. Let's face it; it's tough to see the problem when you don't have another lifestyle to compare it to. Sure, you may have read about a better lifestyle—or you may have relatives who live in a house in a really nice neighborhood—but that is not *your* experience.

I want you to realize that it *can* be your experience. You *can* have a beautiful home in a beautiful neighborhood, you *can* have a great career and earn a lot of money, and you *can* be a true success story! First, you will have to become hopeful. Next, you'll have to look beyond your present circumstances, and then you'll have to *imagine* yourself living a successful life. Once you have started to believe in your dreams, you'll have to open your eyes and learn how to dream with them open.

LESSON LEARNED: Take a few minutes to think about your current situation. What would you like to improve? Now think about some of the dreams that you had when you were younger and the dreams that you have now. Write down anything in your situation that you think can keep you from making your dreams come true. After you have listed all of the things that can keep you from realizing your dreams, I want you to tell yourself the following: "I refuse to let anything stand in the way of my success. There is nothing—absolutely nothing!—that I can't achieve". Now take that list of doubts you created, crumple it up, and toss it in the trashcan where it belongs.

Vision without action is merely a dream.

Action without vision just passes the time.

Vision with action can change the world.

— Joel Barker

Chapter 2

Learning
to Dream

There's nothing more aggravating than having the perfect dream and then waking up. I've even tried to fall back asleep in the hope of returning to the dream world I had been in. It always seems that you wake from these perfect dreams at the most inopportune time—usually just before something really good happens. Eventually, you have to accept the fact that it was only a dream. Well, that's why it's important to learn how to dream with your eyes open. When you dream with your eyes open, you are able to control the dream. You have the power to make the dream a reality. The difference between dreaming with your eyes open and dreaming as we know it is that, when you dream with your eyes open, you start out with the perfect dream or goal, and you don't have to worry about the dream ending before you can really enjoy the good part. You can control the destiny of your dream. The catch is, when you dream with your eyes open, you are responsible for taking actions to make the dream a reality. Otherwise, dreaming with your eyes open bears a striking resemblance to any other dreaming that you can't control. Dreaming with your eyes open without action is merely daydreaming.

Learning to dream with your eyes open may take some getting used to, because, when you dream in a conscious state, you are susceptible to self-doubt. Self-doubt can be crippling. Self-doubt is that little voice that tells you you're not smart enough, you're not good enough, or your goal is unrealistic or requires too much effort. Self-doubt makes you feel totally insecure. It can make you feel hopeless and pessimistic.

Self-confidence can defeat self-doubt. That is why it's important that you build your self-confidence by **a**) reviewing your strengths and accomplishments on a regular basis, **b**) building positive relationships with peers who are working towards their own positive goals, but willing to encourage you if necessary, and **c**) building strong relationships with adults who can help you stay on track. Talk with your parent(s), a favorite teacher, parent of a friend, or any caring adult who can offer sound advice and a good listening ear. Be open to constructive intervention. This type of feedback can help you avoid a dream derailment.

You also have to be able to discern trouble and negative relationships. If you try to hold on to people, places and things that are not aligned with your dreams, you run the risk of wasting your own talents. You run the risk of living in a comatose state where you are able to dream, but nothing ever becomes a reality. Negative outside influences can destroy your dreams. You've got to be able to recognize them, and you've got to be willing to separate yourself from them. One of the hardest parts of dreaming with your eyes open is realizing that you can only dream for yourself. Dreaming with your eyes open is a personal journey. You can't save the world, you can't take everyone with you, and you can't make anyone aspire to be successful. Any attempts at the latter may slow you down or hinder you from reaching your own goals. Instead, do YOU! Let your life be an example for others to follow. Once you've actualized *your* dreams, you'll be in a better position to help others accomplish *theirs*.

Don't be afraid of being different. Don't be afraid of standing out in the crowd. Don't feel guilty if you are the exception to the rule. That's what it takes to be successful. Despite the limited access to resources and opportunities that exist in the Inner City, everyone has an innate ability to survive and overcome the most challenging obstacles. It all boils down to your will and your resilience. How bad do you want it? What are you willing to do to get it? How are you going to handle setbacks and pressure?

The bottom line is, if you're serious about making it, you WILL!! If you can find the confidence to believe that you can live a life that others only dream about, you can make your dreams come true.

LESSON LEARNED: Write down five dreams that you have for your future. Don't feel bad if you haven't figured out how you will make the dreams come true. You are learning to dream with your eyes open. This is just an exercise to help you find personal meaning in the chapter that you just completed. So, take your time and really think about it. What do you want to be when you reach adulthood? What college would you like to attend? What degree do you hope to obtain (Bachelors, Masters, Doctorate)? Where do you want to live? Do you want to own a home? What kind of car do you want to drive? Would you like to visit another country?

After you have written down your dreams, I want you to close your eyes and imagine yourself living the life of your dreams.

Life consists not in holding good cards,

but in playing those you hold well.

— Josh Billings

CHAPTER 3

PLAYING THE CARDS YOU'RE DEALT

I am the younger of two daughters born to a single mother. We lived in the Inner City in a New York City housing project complex. The complex that we lived in is known as one of the worst housing projects in New York City. I don't think that I realized just how poor we were because almost all of my friends and their families lived much the same as we did. Steady employment, two-parent households, owning a car, or not receiving public assistance were all exceptions to the rules in the projects.

Trust me, we were *not* exceptions to those rules. To put the whole thing into perspective, there were times when we only had one light bulb, which my mother would use a towel to unscrew and then transport from her room to ours until we were in bed. After we all said our prayers and "goodnights", she would unscrew the light bulb and take it back to her room.

Although we had a lot in common with the people in our neighborhood, we were raised to see ourselves in a different light. I can remember my mother advising us to be leaders and not followers. She encouraged us to carry ourselves as young ladies and to avoid hanging out with the wrong crowd. She emphasized how important it would be for us to finish high school and "make something of ourselves". She taught us to be proud of our accomplishments and praised each one as if it were more significant than the last. She taught us to be thankful for the things that we did have and was quick to point out that somewhere there was someone who was worse off than we were. Our home environment was structured and filled with love and happiness, so although, in a material sense we were poor, spiritually we were wealthy.

Our zoned school was a few blocks away from where we lived. The day-to-day environment at the school was chaotic. My mother fought with the representatives of the district to get us moved to a school outside of our community. We traveled by school bus to a school with predominately white students. Everything about the school was different...in a good way. The school was cleaner, the halls were quieter, the teachers seemed happier, and the students were more respectful of the rules. The only problem was there weren't many black students who attended. This meant that, in most cases, I was the only black student in my class. I was different.

I don't know where the feeling came from, but I felt that I had a responsibility to be just as good as the other students. I felt as though I had something to prove. Although it was sometimes overwhelming, for some reason I continued to put this pressure on myself. I competed with my own self-doubts until I had built up my self-confidence. I worked hard and involved myself in everything that I could. From spelling bees, to story-telling contests, to school plays, you could bet money that I'd be involved.

It wasn't until high school that I returned to a school in my community. I didn't compete nearly as hard as I should have but still managed to be on track for early graduation. It was at that point—in my senior year—I realized I was about to achieve the only real goal that had been set for me: I was going to graduate from high school. Now, this may surprise some people, but it was pretty uncommon to graduate from high school in the neighborhood where I grew up. I was about to beat the odds, and I was scared to death. What was I going to do? What should I be? What schools should I try to get into?

Unprepared and lacking a plan, I met with the school guidance counselor for advice. He suggested that I attend this great technical college in Upstate New York that offered a hotel management degree. He thought this would be great for me since I had done so well in home economics. Since I did not know of a better option, and I knew a few of the other students who were planning to attend this college, I applied and got accepted.

Here I was, pursuing a goal that someone else had set for me, only to find out a year later that I lacked the passion and interest to complete a degree in hotel management. I ended up changing my major after a year in that program and completed a degree in an area that was altogether different.

This is what happens when you fail to set goals and develop an action plan. If you don't develop a plan, you can end up traveling in a direction that does not best suit your passions, interests, or abilities. You'll lack the ability to make an informed choice or decision about your future. Nonetheless, I am thankful for the advice that I received and the experience. There is something to be gained from every situation.

When I arrived at the college, everything about my new environment was different! The air seemed cleaner, the town was smaller, the nights seemed darker, and the silence was eerie. When you grow up in the Inner City, you become accustomed to noise. But here it was just the opposite; I had to learn how to sleep in dead silence. There were so many new experiences, and I had to adapt quickly.

The college was made up of predominately white students. Most of the people who lived in my dormitory were white. In fact, I can only remember two other black females living on my floor. My roommate was white, and she was tentative (almost fearful!) during our initial meeting. We were from two different worlds, and we had so much to learn about each other. I was a bit disenchanted because I had hoped to room with someone with whom I had more in common. Nonetheless, we both kept open minds and were able to get along well despite our differences.

I can remember one time the look on her face when I returned to the room after perming my hair. She was shocked to see that "the perm did not work". She asked me what had gone wrong, and I wondered the same thing. I mean... my hair was as straight as it could get! It looked fine to me. I couldn't figure out what she saw as "a problem". Then it hit me. If she were to perm *her* hair, she would end up with a head full of curls. But that was not *my* intention. I laughed as I explained to her that where I came from, that would be a Jheri Curl!!!

I returned home for the summer and felt as though I was again in a new environment. But, strangely, nothing had changed. It was almost as if time had stood still since I had gone away. The benches were still filled with young mothers who were engaged in conversation while indulging in the finest malt liquor their money could buy. The dimly lit lobby of the building still smelled of urine and marijuana. The graffiti-covered walls, the elevator door riddled with bullet holes, the floor littered with the remains of White Owls and Phillies cigars, and the windowless window frames and doorless door frames were all signs that I was "home". For some reason, I didn't feel a sense of belonging. I didn't fit in anymore. I was excited about seeing my friends and family, but I couldn't wait to "go back home" to my college dorm.

That summer I received a letter regarding my financial aid. I learned that I would not be receiving the same award I had received the previous year. The reality hit me: I didn't have enough money to return to school! I spoke with several of my school friends who had received the same bad news. For the most part, they decided to take a semester off, work, and save money so that they could return to school the following semester. I was distraught, dejected, and stressed out. Taking off for a semester would mean that I wouldn't be "going home". I'd have to stay in that godforsaken building that used to be my home. I decided not to accept that option.

I returned to school with no money for tuition or room and board. I stood in line to meet with the financial aid advisor. I remember his asking how much money I had to contribute to the financial aid that I *did* receive. I remember the look on his face when I told him that I didn't have any money. He punched away on his adding machine while looking at the papers that I had handed him. He tried to come up with something. It just didn't add up to much. Finally, he told me that there was nothing he could do. The other students on the line were getting restless. Some even expressed their agitation with four-letter words. I was embarrassed. My first reaction was to take my papers and walk away, but then I thought about going back to my old neighborhood. I looked at the advisor with tear-filled eyes and told him that I was not leaving. I told him that I would stand there all day, but he had to figure out something. Fortunately, this was a man who sincerely loved his job; he loved to help people. (I bet the tears may have influenced his reaction a bit, too!) He began to work on the figures again. Finally, he came up with a solution: If I would use the stipend that I received for books and personal expenses to cover the remaining balance for tuition and room and board, I might be able to stay "at home". Without a second thought I agreed. This meant, however, that I would not have any money to purchase the books that my professors had chosen for their respective courses. Nonetheless, it was an option.

I spent many hours in the library completing my assigned reading by poring over the textbooks that were available for use there but could not be taken out. I photocopied pages and pages so that I could keep up with the rest of the class. I never complained to my mother. I always told her that everything was fine. I didn't see a reason to worry her or make her feel guilty. That would have been useless. She was not in a position to offer financial help. I made the best of a bad situation. I found ways to help myself.

The message that this chapter offers is clear: No matter what the situation is, it can be overcome. Sure, there will be obstacles, and many will appear insurmountable on the surface. But you owe it to yourself "to go that extra mile". You owe it to yourself to give your very best.

Many of my friends who decided to take a semester off to save money for college never returned. Who knows what would have happened if they had explored other avenues before giving up? Many of my friends from my old neighborhood still live there today. Many of them are still poverty-stricken, still unemployed, and still stagnant. Who knows what they would be doing if they hadn't succumbed to the societal limitations that were set for them?

No matter how bleak your situation may seem, remember, there is always someone who was worse off than you but decided that failure was not an option. There are a whole lot of people who hold the winning cards and "blow it" because they don't know how to "play the game". Whatever cards end up in your hand, you've got to formulate a plan and execute it. You've got to come up with a winning strategy.

Surprisingly, growing up in "the hood" can actually help you in a lot of ways. Lacking adequate resources or basic necessities enhances your survival skills; you're forced to learn how to improvise. How many times have you decided to make a pitcher of Kool-Aid only to realize that there's not enough sugar? Do you pour out the Kool-Aid and have a glass of water instead? Of course not! You find a way to work it out. So now, instead of a *pitcher* of Kool-Aid, you make a *cup*. Have there been times when your home had no heat? Did you use the oven to warm the place? Did your mom tape plastic over the windows to try to keep the cold air from getting in? Have you ever gotten ready to shower or bathe and realized that there was no hot water? Did you get the biggest pots that you could find and boil water? Have you ever used detergent or dishwashing liquid to add bubbles to your bath water? Have you ever cut open the toothpaste tube to get the last of the toothpaste out? Those are the experiences that give you the skills needed to make the best out of every situation. Those experiences can help you to play whatever cards are in your hand at any given time.

If you throw in the cards, there's no way you can win. But, if you refuse to give up and keep trying to work with the cards you've been dealt, chances are someone else will throw out a card you can use. That can change the dynamics of the game. That can mean the difference between winning and losing.

LESSON LEARNED: Think about the one thing in your life that you see as your greatest obstacle or disadvantage. What do you need to do in order to overcome that obstacle? Write down one experience you have had that has given you the skills you will need to make the best of your situation. Now write down how you plan to overcome that obstacle or disadvantage. Lastly, spend a few minutes reflecting on this quote:

Don't spend so much time worrying about the obstacles; focus on the desired outcome.

Most of the important things in this world have been accomplished by people who kept on trying when there seemed to be no hope at all.

— **Dale Carnegie**

Chapter 4

Beating the Odds

I'm convinced that where you end up in life depends on your level of commitment to whatever you do. Persistence, dedication, and hard work can make or break you. It all depends on whether or not you use them for positive or negative reasons. Some people say that race, economics, and social status determine where a person will end up in life, and, although I agree that those factors can influence the amount of obstacles a person will have to overcome and the work a person has to put in to achieve his/her goals, I've seen too many rich failures and too many poor successes to accept that statement as a pure truth.

Although there is no one specific formula for beating the odds, it'll be pretty tough to overcome anything if you view your situation as hopeless. Instead, look at the overall picture.

- Start out by writing down your goal. Be specific. For example, if your goal is to improve your grades, you're not being specific. If your goal is to improve the "C" that you got in math last quarter to a "B+" by the next grading period, you've made your goal specific. By being specific, it is easier to evaluate whether or not you've attained the goal that you've set for yourself.
- Next, jot down all the negative factors that could keep you from achieving your goals. This list can include people…even you.
- Then jot down potential ways of dealing with each issue. *If you find yourself stuck on a factor that appears to be irresolvable, don't worry. As you begin to work on the surmountable issues, you'll be able to figure out ways to address the tougher ones.*
- Now, make a list of tasks that you need to complete in order to reach your goals.
- Now give yourself the shortest realistic deadline for dealing with each issue and each task.
- Once you have gone through these steps, get started and give it your all.

It is vital for you to realize that the chances of your going through the above steps without any new challenges coming into play are slim to none. Hey, I never said this would be easy. You may need to adjust some of your timeframes—or add new tasks to your original list—but it's manageable. The most important thing is for you to stay focused and committed to achieving your goal. Be ready for failure. Be prepared to confront it head on. Don't worry. Failure isn't final. It too can be overcome.

While growing up in the Inner City, it was common for me to see drug addicts on a daily basis. Many of them were people whom I'd known prior to their addiction. No matter how many drug addicts I came in contact with, their commitment to getting the next "high" never ceased to amaze me. For most of them, the biggest obstacle was that they did not have enough money to purchase the drugs. They were willing to steal from their relatives and friends, beg from strangers, and compromise themselves in the worst ways in order to get the drugs. They didn't care about how they looked, how unpromising the situation looked, or how unrealistic it was to ask someone if they wanted to buy a used pan, old costume jewelry, or a bag of meat. They were willing to do whatever it took in order to reach their goal. They approached the situation with a sense of urgency. They identified what they needed to do in order to get the drugs and stopped at nothing until they were able to get them.

Now imagine what you can accomplish if you put that kind of persistence, dedication, and hard work to *good* use!

LESSON LEARNED: Think about a time that you wanted something and had to really work hard to get it. What did you need to do? Did you have a plan? What obstacles could have kept you from getting what you wanted? How did you get past those obstacles? How does it feel to want something and know that, more than likely, you won't get it? What can you do to see beyond the barrier and work towards a goal that may seem unachievable, but not unrealistic? How does it feel to live in a community where many people never reach their full potential? Why is it important for you to beat those odds?

The greatest danger for most of us is
not that our aim is too high and we miss it,
but that our aim is too low and we reach it.

— Author Unknown

Chapter 5

The Wonder Years

Although this may seem like one of the most difficult periods of your life, with a little effort this can be a very exciting and fulfilling time. Although you're not the kid that you used to be, you are not yet the adult that you are going to be. The good thing is you can actually create the adult that you will become. You can change your life for the better. In order to do so, you have to realize just how important it is to get a good education. Education is the foundation of success. You have to commit to doing your absolute best in every class, on every test, and on every assignment. Set high educational goals for yourself and try your best to exceed them.

I am quite aware that not everyone does as well as they'd like to in every subject, and sometimes that is very discouraging. However, that is not an excuse to accept failure. Study with a peer who does well in the subject that challenges you most. Talk with your teachers on a regular basis and ask them for feedback on your progress in their classes. When they see that you are serious, they will be more than happy to help you accomplish your academic goals. Be sure to ask your teachers for help and additional practice assignments that you can work on in your spare time.

In order to reach your academic goals, you have to realize that you can achieve them. You'll be surprised how much you can improve if you get rid of the self-defeating attitude that has convinced you that you "can't" do better. Keep in mind that you have goals to accomplish, and long-term success is definitely related to academic achievement. If you haven't already started, from now on you've got to get serious about your education. You'll need to make it your priority. You'll need to make a commitment to overall improvement. Even if you're doing well in certain areas, find a way to do better. You'll need to be willing to compete with those on a higher level. This means you'll have to try to do just as good as the top performer in every class. If you work diligently at this goal, your grades will improve significantly. I am aware that being smart is not always viewed as a good thing. For some reason, many inner city youth tend to think that being smart means that you can't be cool. You can do both, but if you've got to choose, consider this: I have never met a person who got into a college or got a job offer because they were cool. I know a whole lot of smart people who did both.

During this stage of your life, you are going through a lot of emotional changes in an effort to fully understand and accept who you are. You are searching for a sense of belonging and may find that you are trying to "fit in" with others or establish friendships or relationships with people who share your interests. This is completely normal.

However, it is important for you to figure out who you are and develop a positive self-concept. How do you see yourself? Do you have a positive or a negative image of your total self? Of course there are things about you that you might want to change, but, overall, do you like being you? When people crack jokes on you or call you names, does it bother you so much that you want to change who you are? Or are you able to laugh at yourself? If you are able to laugh at yourself, you take the power away from the person who is cracking jokes or calling you names. That person wants you to have a negative reaction to what he or she is saying. They want you to feel angry, embarrassed, or inferior. They want to point out your shortcomings in order to hide their own insecurities. Don't give power or credence to such negativity. Learn how to laugh at yourself...and others won't have a reason to laugh anymore.

Knowing who you are can help you set behavior boundaries and avoid following others down the wrong path. We are all influenced by outside factors such as friends, media, entertainers, and role models, but it is important for each of us to have our own set of ideals. Knowing who you are and accepting who you are will make it easier to get through "the Wonder Years". It will minimize the impact of peer pressure, improve your self-esteem (the way you feel about yourself), and help you to develop leadership characteristics.

Yes, these are "the Wonder Years" and they'll be full of opportunities for academic and social growth. Make the most of these years. Make them memorable. Make them wonderful.

LESSON LEARNED: Write down a change you will make beginning today that will help you to improve academically and/or behaviorally at school. Do you need to spend more time studying? Do you have to catch up with assigned readings? Do you talk in class? Do you need to adjust your attitude a little bit? Do you need additional help in a particular subject? Now, write down three positive characteristics that you possess. That is, three things that define who you are and set you apart from other people.

We must believe that we are gifted for something,

and that this thing, at whatever cost,

must be attained.

— Marie Curie

CHAPTER 6

WHAT'S YOUR MOTIVATION?

What makes you tick? What is it that really gets you going? That's what you've got to figure out. Once you figure out what will motivate you to achieve success, ride the wave. It may not get you all the way to your goal, but it'll definitely get you closer. You're probably wondering why motivation may not get you to success, and the answer is simple. Motivation may not get you to success because—like a wave—motivation is temporary. Once it's gone, you've got to run out and find a new one.

Feeling like I had something to prove—and feeling that it was my responsibility to excel in grade school because of the limited number of African Americans enrolled in the gifted program—motivated me during my elementary and junior high school years.

But that motivation was gone once I started high school. My environment was different, I had friends from my community, and I didn't feel pressured to work as hard as I had worked before. I was a young adult who was dealing with the complexities of adolescence and forced to face the day-to-day chaos in my neighborhood.

I was more concerned than ever before about boys, fitting in, and fashionable clothing. I didn't once feel like I was compromising my goal because I knew it was achievable. I just didn't set any new ones for myself, so I didn't really feel like I needed motivation. Not for school anyway.

There was so much turmoil in my community. So many of my young friends were dying senseless deaths as a result of gun violence and drugs. Getting caught up in crossfire was becoming the norm. Not many nights went by without the sound of gunfire ripping through the air. Attending funeral services for young friends had become routine. That's what led to my next motivation.

I had gone to so many funerals, and, after the tears dried, life just went on. It was as if everyone forgot that that person ever existed. I remember feeling that, since death was as certain as life, I needed to make sure that, if I died, it would matter. I wanted to be remembered. I wanted to leave a legacy. In the least,

I wanted my obituary to reflect my importance. Call it morbid, but it helped me get to college. A strong desire to get out of my neighborhood helped me make it through college. And the further I got, the more I realized that the possibilities were endless.

I am constantly adjusting my goals and motivation based on my circumstances. When it seemed that I might not be able to achieve the work-related goals that I set for myself because the educational requirements called for a higher degree than the one I held, I returned to school. When the landlord complained about my son running on the floor, I was motivated to set a homeownership goal. When I heard that Oprah Winfrey had planned to give up the Oprah Winfrey Show in five years, I panicked. That meant that I only had a short time to make something big happen, something big enough to get me on the Oprah Winfrey Show before the final curtain call. Although five years have come and gone since I first heard that rumor, that still motivates me!!

So, although your motivation may seem silly to other people, it's yours. If it works for you, then it has served its purpose. What motivates one person may not mean a thing to another person. Find your motivation. Make it work for you, and when it doesn't work for you anymore, find a new one.

LESSON LEARNED: Most people are motivated by fear/punishment, incentive/reward, recognition, or values/principles. Choose the most appropriate response so that you can get an idea of your motivational pattern.

I usually do my chores because:

_____ If I don't, I will get in trouble (f)

_____ I want to get my allowance (i)

_____ My parent(s) tell me how happy it makes them (r)

_____ Keeping the house clean and neat is important to me (v)

I do my homework because:

_____ If I don't, my parents will yell (f)

_____ My teacher assigned it, and I have to follow rules (v)

_____ I don't want to be the only one who doesn't have it if the teacher checks (r)

_____ I won't get my allowance if I don't (i)

I try to get good grades in school because:

_____ I want to be on the honor roll or get an award (r)

_____ I usually get a present when I get good grades (i)

_____ I always want to do my best (v)

_____ If I don't, I won't be able to watch TV, use the telephone, or go outside (f)

If I disrespected my parents:

_____ I would probably get a beating (f)

_____ I might get to live with my favorite aunt (i)

_____ It might make them listen to what I have to say (r)

_____ I would feel like I let them down (v)

I want to graduate from college because:

_____ I want to be successful (v)

_____ I know that my parents and family would be proud (r)

_____ If I don't, my parents would probably throw me out of the house (f)

_____ I'll probably get a gift from my parents when I graduate (i)

I am reading this book because:

_____ Everybody else is reading it (r)

_____ I want to learn how to become successful (v)

_____ I will get a reward when I complete it (i)

_____ My parent(s) or teacher said that I have to, and if I don't I'll get in trouble (f)

At the end of each statement is a letter. Fear = (f), Recognition/Achievement = (r), Incentive = (i), and Values = (v). Count up the number of times you used each letter. Which did you use the most? Which did you use the least? The letter that you used the most indicates your motivational pattern. For example, if you have four f's, you probably do what you are supposed to do because you are afraid of the consequences of not doing what you are told. If you have more r's, then you probably do what you are supposed to do because you like for people to notice what you've accomplished. If most of your responses fit in the v category, you are probably motivated by the morals, beliefs and principals instilled by your parents, relatives, teachers and/or other caring adults. If you find that most of your responses were from the i category, you probably respond quicker when there is something material to be gained. You are inspired to perform when you know that you will receive some type of reward.

Although, we are all motivated by different things at different times, it's important to know exactly what it takes to make us give our best performance. Find your motivation for every challenge that life presents.

If you can find a path with no obstacles,

it probably doesn't lead anywhere.

— Frank A. Clark

CHAPTER 7

CHANGING LANES

You may start out with a goal and, after working towards it, come to realize that it is not what you want to accomplish at all. This can be one of the most confusing and frustrating experiences you'll ever have. On the one hand, you've come so close to reaching a milestone; but on the other hand, you're now realizing that there is something that is more interesting and more meaningful than your initial objective.

Well, if you come to this point, it's okay. Just take the time to evaluate the reasons or circumstances that have led to your decision. If you're changing your course because it's just too difficult or goal attainment is just too far away, then you may not be changing for a good reason. Don't let self-doubt slip in and wreak havoc on your plans. Don't give up because success seems too far away. Remember, at this point you're closer to success than you've ever been before. You may need to adjust your plan or approach a bit, but you can still accomplish your goal. However, if you reflect on the objective and find that your aspirations no longer match the intended outcome, it's okay to set a new goal. It's never too late to change directions.

Approach the new goal with caution. You'll definitely run into obstacles again. It may take even longer to see the success you're expecting, so make sure that you establish a realistic time frame for achieving your goal. Once you make the "educated" decision to change your goal, step on it. Get over into the new lane before the reality of your present circumstances causes you to change your mind. The worst thing that can happen is you get stuck in traffic in a lane that is not going to take you where you are trying to go.

So many people are stuck in their own personal traffic jams, traveling on dead-end streets, driving without a road map, and running out of gas. They know that the road ahead is leading nowhere but are afraid to adjust the plan. As a result, they continue ahead in dead-end jobs, unhealthy relationships, and unpleasant circumstances. Although the road doesn't offer any promise, it is familiar. It feels safe. The problem is, when you don't aggressively pursue your goals, you'll always wonder what would've happened if you did. You may be able to find some good things about the path you decided to remain on, but for the most part, you'll still feel incomplete.

I recently came across an interesting quote by Dietrich Bonhoeffer, a theologian. He said "If you board the wrong train, it's no use running along the corridor in the opposite direction." It doesn't matter how fast you run, you'll still end up some place that you don't want to be. You have to get off the train to get to where you are trying to go.

It took 35 years for my mother to move out of the projects. Although she was not happy about her circumstances, she had learned to live with them. She had spent so much time convincing herself that she couldn't do any better, she had come to accept her reality as her destiny. She let self-doubt and "what ifs" control her life. Her foot was always on the brake; she was in the wrong lane and going nowhere. I watched her put her all into a dead-end job that couldn't even pay the bills. She learned to operate with a constant deficit and was content to just have food to eat, a roof over her head, and a job that could help her get through each day. She valued the security of subsidized housing, even if it meant that she had to deal with broken elevators, dark stairwells, occasional gunfire, and strangers lurking in the lobby. I tried to pull her foot off the brake pedal so many times. I tried to chart out a course for her and give her a road map to success. It was useless. She was too afraid of uncertainty.

One year after I had relocated to another state and purchased a home, my mother came to visit. She was overwhelmed by the situation. To say that she was elated is an understatement. She walked around the house as if she were dreaming. Although I knew I had so much more to accomplish, I had achieved more than my mother had ever imagined.

I tried to convince her to relocate and start anew, but to no avail. At some points it seemed I broke down the wall of resistance, but her tools of self-doubt were constantly working to build it back up. When it was time for her to return home, she noticed my disappointment and agreed that she would contemplate relocating in five years. For me, that was no consolation, but there was nothing that I could do. Only she had the ability to change her situation.

Shortly after she returned home, she called to tell me that she was relocating within the next two months. I was ecstatic!! After years of my trying to pry her foot off the brake, she had taken a quick look back and decided to get into a new lane!

I asked her what changed her mind, and she told me that, when she returned home and saw all of the people hanging out in the lobby, and the peeling paint in her bedroom that had not been repaired in years, she felt disgusted. She said she wanted to get out of there as soon as possible.

You see, because she had accepted her situation, she had stopped looking for another path. She adapted to her environment and learned to make the best of the worst. She was hopeless. She couldn't see any new possibilities because she was looking straight ahead on a dead-end street. Exposure to a new environment helped her find the courage that she needed to venture out on a new course.

Whatever it is that you need to change in order to grow, change it. Growth necessitates change.

LESSON LEARNED: Think about something in your life that you really need to change. Perhaps you've been making unhealthy food choices and find that you are a little overweight. Maybe you've been failing a class and haven't really done enough to improve your grade. Maybe you've stopped going to classes or find yourself in a program for troubled youth. It could be as simple as your choice of friends—do you have any friends who aren't on a positive track and could be heading for failure? Can you identify what it is that is keeping you from making the needed change? Once you have identified the roadblock, write it down. Next, write down why making the change is more important than remaining in your current situation. Lastly, spend a few minutes reflecting on this quote:

Sometimes you have to change your mind

in order to change your life.

What I do today is important,

for I'm exchanging a day of my life for it.

— Author Unknown

CHAPTER 8

DECISIONS, DECISIONS, DECISIONS

As if growing up in the Inner City were not tough enough, you'll also have to make your own decisions. Although there are some controls in place to help us avoid total destruction, such as parents, teachers, counselors, clergy, government, law enforcement, and the like, it all boils down to choice and free will. We all have the power to make choices. The choices that you make can affect your life and the lives of countless others. So you've got to commit to making responsible choices from now on. Don't wait until someone else has to tell you what to do. That will only make you resentful and could cause you to rebel against something that is right but you're just not "feeling" it because of the way the person approached the situation. You see, most of the time rebellion stems from the feeling that someone is infringing on your independence. Well, if you know what is right, and you do it on your own, you'll never have to worry about anyone telling you what to do. Making the "right" decision is not always easy. For one thing, sometimes you don't know what is "right" and what is "wrong". When this happens, think about outcomes and consequences and do what is "best".

Other times, you'll have to trust your instinct. Have you ever walked down the street and had a feeling that you should take a different route than the one you usually take? Have you ever had a feeling that something bad was about to happen? Have you ever had the feeling that you should or shouldn't do something? That's instinct. It's a strong gut feeling, a sixth sense. Believe me, it can save your life.

I'm sure that you've already been in situations where you had to make tough choices. There are so many outside influences in the Inner City that force young people to deal with adult situations. In some cases you'll have to deal with things that your parents never even had to think about. You probably chose not to talk to your parents about some of the things you deal with on an everyday basis because you know they would never understand. If this is your reality, you're going to have to rely on any and every positive influence you've been exposed to in order to get through some of the challenges of growing up in the Inner City.

Some of the important social challenges that you're either dealing with or about to deal with are gang involvement, sex, drugs, alcohol, and peer pressure. No matter what controls are in place, you're going to have to make some decisions around these issues. It's unavoidable.

Now, most adults will just tell you not to get involved in anything negative. It's just that simple. I'm not convinced that it's as easy as we adults suggest. It's hard to be in the "in crowd" when you're not indulging in any negative activities. It's hard to walk away from the "in crowd" when these are the people you've grown up with. You know that they're not bad people, because you're around them all the time. You may even feel as if you can hang around with this crowd without being involved in the negativity. Maybe you can, but why? You'll feel awkward and out of place, or you'll feel some pressure to engage in the activity. The easiest way to avoid this is to do a quick assessment. Ask yourself "What's in this for me?" "How can this *help* me get to where I need to go?" "How can this *keep* me from getting to where I need to go?" "Is this worth the risk involved?" If you know what you're trying to achieve—and you know what it takes to get there—then you know that, no matter how tough the decision is, it's up to you to do the right thing for yourself.

I can't think of a better time to tell you about a dear relative of mine. He too grew up in the projects. His father was serving a 15-year prison sentence, which left his mother to raise him and his brother alone. His mother had a good job and was able to provide the necessities for the family, and she was also able to provide them with the things that they wanted. These were the children who were lucky enough to have a new bicycle, toys, games, allowance, and fashionable clothes. They were raised in a Christian home where there were rules and structure, but they were allowed to hang out with friends, go to parties, and socialize.

Since I am a few years younger than my relative, I am not exactly sure where his life took a negative turn. I can only tell you that he started hanging out with the wrong crowd, gained a reputation as a thug, had unprotected sex, became a teenage father, started using drugs, and eventually became addicted. The rest was completely downhill.

He was involved in a situation in which a robbery occurred that resulted in the death of a retired police officer. While he admits to consenting to rob the man, he denies that there was ever any intention of murdering him. Things just went completely wrong. Although he maintained that he was not the shooter, he was charged with murder. He refused to "point the finger" at the triggerman because he was not a "snitch" and couldn't imagine "selling out". Since he and one of his peers refused to tell what happened, they were both charged with murder. A third accomplice testified against my relative and, in exchange, was given a three-year sentence.

My relative was convicted and sentenced at the age of 18 and is currently serving 31 years to life. (His son, who was one year old at that time, has already graduated from high school!) Barring a miracle, he still has 11 years left before becoming eligible for parole. And there's no guarantee that he will be released when he is finally granted a parole hearing.

You see, before this situation went completely out of control, there were so many opportunities for him to change lanes or make a different choice. It just became more difficult. He could've chosen not to drop out of high school or could've completed the requirements for a General Equivalency Diploma. He could've decided not to use drugs or at least sought help to deal with his addiction. He could've decided to abstain from sexual activity until he was ready to take on the responsibilities that come with that or could have decided not to engage in unprotected sex. He could've chosen not to be a part of the robbery that fateful night or at least given the entire story to the authorities upon questioning. There's so much room to correct a mistake, to regroup and salvage your future, but the feeling of hopelessness or the severity of the situation can cloud your vision.

Since incarceration, this individual has gone from a boy to a man, from drug dependency to living a drug-free life. He's gone from high school dropout to college graduate, and has gone from being irresponsible and downright reckless to teaching youth about the importance of making good choices and the life-changing impact of negative ones. If he is able to make these positive contributions to society from behind bars, just imagine what he could have offered to society had he made better choices and decisions as an adolescent.

As an adolescent, he had the responsibility to make decisions and choices that were sometimes on an adult level. The irony is, now he doesn't even have the opportunity to decide whether or not he will go outside, what he will wear, how much food he can receive from family, or how many people can visit him and on which days they can visit. I implore you to learn from the mistakes of others so that you can avoid the fate that they are forced to live with. If you don't make good choices and decisions, you'll also lose the privilege.

I'm willing to bet that you'll be offered drugs and/or the chance to sell them, invited to join a gang, or approached about having sex. Some of these prospects might appear rather enticing on the surface, but you've got to use the processes and steps that we talked about so far to get through them.

I'm sure you know people who tell you that smoking weed or drinking alcohol is not bad. They may even suggest that marijuana should be legalized. The problem is, they both impair your judgment, and you need to have good judgment to make good decisions. Marijuana and alcohol alter your mood, and that can make you participate in things you would never otherwise have considered if you had not been under their influence. Take a look at the people around you who smoke marijuana or drink alcoholic beverages. What does it look like they get out of it? Are they living the life that you want to live?

It might seem cool to join a gang, especially when you have several friends who are in the gang. You've probably hung around with the gang from time to time, and they may even "look out" for you. As an outsider, you might long for the sense of belonging that the gang offers. Again, you've got to assess the situation. What are the consequences? That's the biggest question you have to deal with when you're considering gang involvement. Do you really want to be a part of a group that requires you jeopardize your life, your character, or your future? There are a lot of groups and organizations that you *can* join if you're searching for something to "belong" to. Start out with the groups, clubs and sports that are offered at your school and within the community. If that's not a viable option, you'll need to find a mentor. A mentor is a person who is living a positive lifestyle and contributing to the society in which we live. A mentor is a role model, a person worth emulating. Think about the people who are presently involved in your life. Is there anyone who takes an interest in what you're doing? Is there anyone who is concerned about your success? Do you feel comfortable talking about tough issues with anyone in particular? That person would probably be more than happy to take on the responsibility of a mentor.

Sex seems to be one of the toughest issues for young people to deal with and for many reasons. First of all, if you're like most young people, you probably have at least one close friend who has engaged in sexual activity and told you all about it. I'm sure that his/her account of the story has made you more interested in sex. But who can you ask? Most adults will tell you not to do it, but you probably feel as if they haven't given you a good reason why you shouldn't do it. You know for certain that your parents had to do it to get you here, so why shouldn't you do it?

Well, here is one of those areas where you're able to make your own decision. There are laws in place that keep young people from driving a car until a certain age. There's even a legal drinking age. But even when laws are in place, there are constant violations. When it comes to sex, there are no legal consequences (except prosecution for statutory rape—and that's a consequence for an adult who engages in sexual activity with a minor) that serve as a deterrent to sexual involvement. So, it's up to you. First of all, **Who** is the person that you want to have sex with? *Not just his/her name, but what is this individual about?* What are his/her future plans? What is he/she into? **What** are the consequences and risks involved? **When** it's over, will this person respect you? **Where** is the relationship with this person going? **Why** can't it wait? **How** could this affect your future? After you've answered these questions, wait at least one month before you make your decision.

You're probably thinking that this is not realistic. Not only is it realistic, it's absolutely necessary. Why? Because important decisions require assessment, reasoning, and time. You've got to be sure that you're not making a big mistake. Most bad decisions are spontaneous, involve very little thought or reasoning, and lead to regrets.

During the one-month waiting period, do some research on gonorrhea, syphilis, chlamydia, genital herpes, genital warts and HIV/AIDS. You need to be well informed about the possible consequences of your actions. Young people are dying of AIDS in record numbers, and you have no way of knowing if a person is infected with HIV/AIDS just by looking at them. And that's just one of many sexually transmitted diseases you need to be concerned about.

Also do some research on teenage pregnancy and how it impacts the lives of both partners. If you find yourself intrigued by the idea of being a parent, figure out what fascinates you the most. Is it the idea of dressing the baby in the "phatest" outfits? Is it the idea of buying him or her the latest sneakers? Is it the idea of having someone to call your own? Are you searching for someone to love you unconditionally?

Well, think about the cost involved in raising a child. Think about the sacrifices you'll have to make. Think about the emotional support a child needs. What happens when the novelty has worn off and the baby needs Pampers, but you need a new pair of shoes or sneakers? What happens if you want to go away to college but can't because you have a baby to care for? Are you able to provide for the emotional, social, and financial well-being of a child? How will becoming a teenage parent affect your goals and dreams?

Ask your partner the Who, What, When, Where, Why and How questions that you had to an-swer. Then, ask him/her to tell you why he/she wants to have a sexual relationship with you. Find out how many people that person has had sex with. Ask if he/she has ever had unprotected sex. Ask this person to tell you what he/she likes or "loves" about you. Finally, ask how he/she would respond if you decide that you aren't ready to have sexual intercourse. If this individual can't answer these questions, you can't answer these questions, or you're afraid to ask the questions, it might be an indication that either one or both of you are not mature enough to deal with a sexual relationship at this point. In any case, after a month you might feel differently about this person and/or the situation. Abstinence is the best answer, but no matter what you decide, unprotected sex is NOT an option.

It's so easy to get into trouble and so hard to get out of it. One bad decision usually requires another. So it's best not to make a bad one. Peer pressure is extremely stressful and hard to resist. If you make the right decisions, you may be ostracized by some of your peers, or your partner may move on to someone else who's "ready". You've got to be willing to accept that. True friends or partners will support your decision to do the right thing...even if they decide not to. Of course, they may try to encourage you to do whatever it is that they are doing, but they'll be willing to respect your decision when they realize how important it is to you. If not, you'll have to move on. Don't be concerned about "keepin' it real" with everyone else; you've got to be concerned about "keepin' it real" with yourself. You've got a plan, and you can't compromise it for anyone.

LESSON LEARNED: Think about a time that you made a poor choice that resulted in a negative consequence. Who was affected by the decision you made? Did you disappoint someone you love? Did you let yourself down? If you could do it all over again, what would you do differently? What are some of the things that you have to deal with on a regular basis that require you to make tough decisions? Why is it important for you to make the right decision every time? How do you plan to avoid negative influences that can ruin your dreams?

IMPOSSIBLE:

What no one can do, until someone does.

— Author Unknown

Chapter 9

From Impossible to I'm Possible

I've found that some people spend way too much time thinking about why they can't achieve a goal and not enough time on making it happen. Often the reason is because the person lacks self-confidence. The lack of self-confidence has killed a lot of dreams. In order to do anything you have to believe that it can be done. You also have to fight off the feeling of inferiority. There are a lot of successful people who never ever went to college. Some never even completed high school! The one thing they all have in common is that at some point they began to believe they could do whatever it was they set out to do. Once they found a way to believe in themselves, they had to take action. Taking action is just as important as believing that you can accomplish something. There are countless people who believe they can do something with their lives but don't want to put in the effort required to achieve the goal. Or even worse, they begin to put in the effort but give up before they reach the finish line. When you're on the road to success, you can't stop to lament that your life is tougher than the next man's. You can't sit around and feel sorry for yourself. There's just no time. You'll be run over by someone who is serious about success.

Perhaps you are motherless or fatherless, poor or misunderstood. You may have been abused or may *still* be living in an abusive household. Maybe someone in your family is a drug addict or you don't have food to eat. You may be missing a limb, suffering from an illness, depressed, or have some negative history that you feel will make it impossible for you to "make it". Understandably, these are serious and difficult issues to deal with, but they too can be overcome. Ponder this:

- Magic Johnson is HIV positive but hasn't let that stop him from pursuing business ventures that help to revive urban neighborhoods and offer their residents opportunities for economic growth.
- Oprah Winfrey grew up in poverty and was sexually abused as a child, but she didn't let either of those things keep her from setting and attaining her goals.

- Frederick Douglas couldn't read or write and had to teach himself.
- Tom Cruise grew up poor and suffered from a learning disability.
- Harriet Tubman found her way to freedom and risked her life to free other slaves.
- Sammy Sosa grew up in poverty. He had to sell juice and shine shoes for spare change in order to help his mom. He couldn't afford a baseball bat or glove, so he made a bat out of a tree branch and used a milk carton to make a glove. And the baseball? He made that by rolling socks together and putting tape on them.
- Former President Bill Clinton grew up poor and lived in an unhealthy environment in which his step dad abused his mother.
- Ray Charles lost his eyesight at the age of seven, but didn't let that stop him from pursuing his dream.
- Throughout childhood, Dr. Antonia Novello suffered a painful chronic illness of the colon. After undergoing a corrective surgery during her junior year in college, she had to wear diapers to classes for six months! She didn't let that stop her. She went on to become the first Hispanic and first female Surgeon General of the United States.
- Tina Turner was a victim of domestic violence and often performed on stage after being beaten.

- Vanessa Williams was the first African-American to be crowned "Miss America" and was later forced to give up the title after nude pictures of her appeared in *Penthouse* magazine. She went on to become a great actress and singer.
- Ellen Ochoa was raised in a single parent household and became NASA's first Hispanic female astronaut.
- Marshall Mathers ("Eminem") grew up poor and lived in a trailer park. He had a difficult time being accepted in the rap game because he is white, but he believed in his dream and wouldn't take "No" for an answer.
- Venus and Serena Williams grew up in a poverty-stricken, inner city community.

What do all of those famous people have in common? Although their struggles were different, the answer is the same: they were all able to overcome adversity and make their mark on the world.

If they were able to accomplish their goals, why shouldn't you be able to accomplish yours? Instead of dwelling on your shortcomings, figure out what it is that you are good at, and find a way to succeed. Don't minimize your talents, because there is someone out there who is making a living using some of the very skills that you take for granted. Perhaps you can sing, cook, draw, write, speak well, or have a natural mathematical ability. Maybe you've cut open a frog in biology and didn't feel like you were about to puke. Maybe you're really good at decorating or putting together the perfect outfit. You may be really good at convincing other people to do things your way. Think about the number of careers that you can explore just using those skills, talents and abilities!!

There are hidden talents and job opportunities in everything that you do! Are you a video game junky? Well, there are jobs that require someone to create the games, and there are also people who are paid to test the games. So, maybe instead of just sitting around playing games for fun, you can start doing some research and figuring out how you can make a career out of it. The best job will be one that you love to do. So when you think about a career, try and figure out a few things that you would do even if there were no pay involved. If you can find a career that is satisfying without a monetary incentive, you'll never feel like you're "working".

Volunteer work and interning are two important tasks that you need to immediately get involved in. These tasks will expose you to different environments and, more importantly, put you in contact with people who will be able to help you reach your goals. It's a good idea to volunteer or intern in a place where you can learn more about a particular field that you are interested in. This may help you decide whether you will continue to pursue work or a career in the area related to your experience, or if you want to explore other career interests before settling on one. Either way, you'll have an opportunity to work directly with people who make a living doing the kind of work that you are considering. You can ask them questions about the job, observe the work that is being done, and learn more about the responsibilities and the rewards attached to that field.

It may be easier to find an organization in your neighborhood that needs volunteers than it will be to find an organization that is looking for an intern. So, start out as a volunteer. Determine how many hours of service you can give to the organization, and be careful not to take on more than you can handle. Although this is strictly an unpaid work experience, you'll need to perform every project as if you were being paid. Strong work ethics can lead to incredible opportunities. If you are seen as a responsible worker, you could end up with a part-time or summer job with the same organization. One thing for certain, you'll always be able to get a letter of recommendation or a reference from the person you worked with. Trust me, a good word is priceless. It can be the deciding factor in whether or not you get into the college or university that you want to attend, or it can help you land the perfect job.

Finding a good place to do an internship is a

bit of a challenge, because it means that the company must assign a representative to help you achieve your goals as well. Often employers just don't have the time or the resources to dedicate to such a project. Nonetheless, there are many employers who work with upper high school and college level interns. It's your job to find one that matches your area of interest. A good place to start researching internships is the local library. There are some really good books that list employers who offer internships. You can also find out the requirements, application dates and deadlines, and any other information that the employer lists. Since some employers only accept applications for internships once or twice each year, you should begin to research possible internship opportunities a year ahead of time. Be prepared to explain—both in writing and verbally—why you want the internship.

If a top company has an internship program, you can bet your bottom dollar that it is extremely competitive. Sometimes there are only one or two openings for an intern, and hundreds of students apply for the opportunity. Your job is to make sure that you do everything possible to ensure that you are one of the two people selected.

If you keep a positive attitude and are willing to put in the work, success is achievable. In fact, it's inevitable! Don't let anyone tell you that your dreams are not realistic or that the odds are not in your favor.

You can be a doctor, lawyer, actor, baseball player, engineer, architect, journalist, sports commentator, singer, veterinarian, astronaut, gymnast, talk show host, business owner, accountant, teacher…or anything else you choose to be. You just have to want it bad enough. You have to realize that you can do it. You have to make it your mission.

When I graduated from Delhi College, I thought that I had enough education to move into the "real world". I enthusiastically wrote my resume and started looking for a job. I made sure that I purchased the Sunday edition of the New York Times, because I was advised that this was the best edition for job seekers. Although I sent out at least twenty resumes each week, I rarely received a request for additional information or an interview. Whenever I did get the call to meet with someone, I would have to borrow an interview appropriate outfit. I also had trouble maintaining enough money for car fare and postage to mail out the resumes.

It took a while for me to come to terms with the fact that I did not have the skills or education that employers were looking for. Once I admitted that fact to myself, I began looking for a job in fields that did not require a degree or much experience such as telemarketing, cashiering, and temporary work assignments through employment agencies. Eventually I got a part-time job at a movie theater. I had to take two buses to get to work and made a little bit more than minimum wage.

Here I was, a college graduate, working in the very same movie theatre that I absolutely refused to work at while in high school. The theater was frequented by teenagers who lived in my neighborhood and initially I felt embarrassed every time someone I knew walked through the door. I wore a purple polyester skirt, lavender shirt, and purple polyester bow-tie. Believe me; you would not have wanted to wear that uniform.

After a few weeks on the job, I started to feel better about it. I started to look at it from a positive perspective. Working part-time at the movie theater allowed me to:

- have enough money to help out with household expenses
- save money for postage for mailing resumes
- spend the day-time hours job searching and networking
- set aside money for carfare whenever I had an interview
- gain invaluable work experience
- realize that I didn't have to be embarrassed about earning money for an honest day of work

Not long after I started working at the theater, I got another part-time job at a youth program across the street from where I lived. I worked both jobs and began to feel pretty good about my situation. I worked as an intake worker at the youth center and didn't have too much responsibility. I just had to make sure that anyone who came into the building signed the log. After about a week, I was bored to death. Instead of quitting the job, I found a way to make it fit my needs. I helped out with organized games, started a weekly youth rap session, spent time finding out what the youth were interested in doing, and planned a fashion/talent show.

It didn't take long for the Director to notice the bond I was developing with the youth. He offered me a summer position as a supervisor for the summer camp program. This job nearly doubled my pay rate. Things were finally looking up and I was able to quit the job at the movie theater. I was grateful for the chance to supervise a youth program and felt quite content with how things were turning out. I had a job that I liked and was earning a decent pay. I considered the fact that I lived across the street and didn't have to spend money on carfare an extra bonus.

I worked really hard and made it a point to do more than he expected. I wanted to secure a place for myself at the youth center. One day, the Director called me into his office and asked if I had a resume.

I gave him a copy and he told me that he was going to make a few changes that might improve my marketability. He told me that he saw so much potential in me and that I needed to be doing bigger things. I was a little confused and asked him if that meant that I would not have a job after the summer. He told me that I did not need to worry because I could work there as long as the program had funding, but that he didn't feel it would be in my best interest. He explained that there were no positions there that would propel me to the next level and that he felt I was ready for growth. Just when I thought I had arrived, he told me it was time to move on. He had more confidence in my ability than I did. My stomach turned, my heart beat accelerated, and I was at a loss for words.

When he gave me the new version of my resume, I could not believe my eyes! It was so much more professional. It was as if he had written about another person, but it was all about me. Everything was true, but it sounded a whole lot better than the resume that I had given him. That resume helped me to get my first "real" full-time job. I was hired by the New York City Department of Corrections as a Correctional Counselor.

In order to get there, I had to start out in a less desirable job and work my way up. I also had to be open to the constructive intervention of someone with more experience in the world of work. Nine times out of ten, that's the way it happens.

When you start out on your personal mission, it might seem like an impossible task. Keep working towards it. The more you work, the more realistic the goal will seem. Before you know it, you'll have the confidence you need to take your goal to the next level. Before you know it, you'll be able to see the finish line. Before you know it, the impossible will have occurred. So stop seeing the world through negative eyes. Try to approach situations from a realistic but optimistic perspective. Learn to focus on the potential in yourself.

From now on, find a way to accept the fact that anything is possible...especially *you!*

LESSON LEARNED: Make a list of the things that you are good at. Are you a fast runner? Are you a good ball handler? Do you have an excellent memory? Are you a great listener? Are you really funny? Are you a math whiz? Can you write poetry or rap lyrics? Do you have a great singing voice? Are you a good artist? Are you good at following directions? Do you seem to always know what to say to make people feel better? Are you good at arguing your point or the point of others? Can you play an instrument? Do you like to fix things? Do you know a little bit about working on cars? These are just a few ideas; your talents and abilities may be completely different. Think about jobs that might require your talents and write them down. If you can't think of them all, ask others who care about you to help you. Parents, relatives and friends may be able to point out talents that you overlook. Teachers and counselors will be able to offer you advice and guidance related to careers that match your talents. Next, write down two places that you would like to volunteer in your community and the reasons why for each. Think about a few entry-level jobs that you would like to do before you get started with a career job. Remember, entry-level jobs will be an important step on your journey to success. You'll learn valuable work ethics that will prepare you for your career job. Now take a few minutes and think about the meaning of the following quote:

By expanding our deepest beliefs about what is possible, we change our experience of life.

— Dan Millman

To be without some of the things you want

is an indispensable part of happiness.

— **Bertrand Russell**

Chapter 10

All About the Benjamins

In the inner city communities there is a tendency to spend rather than to save. Part of the reason for this is that quite often the adults in the community are struggling to make ends meet. In this case, the dilemma then becomes: How do you save when you're in debt? How do you save when the refrigerator's empty? How do you save when you don't even have enough money to go to the laundromat? How do you save for a rainy day when the sun just refuses to shine? I understand!!! It was difficult for my mom to save because, by the time she received her check, she would owe most of the money to a relative or friend. She was determined to pay off her debts (even when it meant that she would have less money for groceries).

However, even in this situation, saving is possible.

The first thing you need to do is establish a budget. A budget is an itemized list of all of your expenses and a breakdown of all of the money that you will receive. Some people set up their budgets based on their pay schedule (weekly, bi-weekly). Another way to set up a budget is based on when the bills are due.

Once you set up a budget, you get a clear picture of how you can make changes in your spending pattern that will result in savings. You will be able to see how many things you spend money on that are "wants" and how many things you spend money on for your "needs". After you identify the total amount of money that you spend on "wants" (junk food, cable television, fast food, etc.), you will have to decide what you are willing to eliminate in order to save for things that are important to you.

You're probably thinking, "I don't pay bills" or "I don't buy groceries". Well, even if you are not paying bills, you can prepare for financial success. This is an area where you can take a proactive approach. You can help your adult family and friends by sharing this information with them. Now, be careful; this can be difficult. If your parent(s) are anything like my mom, they probably won't be open to your advice at first. Start out by creating a household budget. Ask them to help. Let them know that you are working on a project and would like to use real information. Separate "wants" from "needs" in the budget and suggest some small changes. For example, limit the number of snacks purchased. At the grocery store utilize coupons, or replace one brand food item with a store brand item each time you shop. Whatever money you manage to save is the start of your family's new savings plan.

If your parent(s) don't cooperate, there may be other ways for you to get in the habit of saving money. Consider this:

- Most inner city youth spare no expense to keep up with the latest fashion trends—from jewelry, sneakers, jerseys, hats and jeans, to shoes, shades, belts, purses and backpacks!!! Are you wearing your savings?
- Most inner city youth spend money on food outside of the home. How often during the week do you stop at Mickey Dees, the local Chinese restaurant, or the neighborhood deli for a hero/sub? Are you eating your savings?
- Many inner city youth spend money on the latest gadgets such as the most up-to-date cell phone or two-way pager. Are you talking away your savings?

...And I bet you thought that there was no way that you could save any money!!! There's always a way. You just need to focus on what is important and make a commitment to save. You see, fashion trends change and gadgets quickly become outdated. In fact, most material possessions lose value immediately after you buy them.

As you mature, the ability to manage money will become more and more critical. So it is important for you to develop good money management skills now. If you do anything long enough, it becomes a part of you. It becomes a habit.

After you figure out how much you can save, set a financial goal. Save towards something important (Mother's Day, the prom, your best friend's birthday, college). Start to pay attention to your spending patterns. Be able to account for every dime that you receive. Write down everything that you spend money on. You should keep an index card in your wallet, purse, backpack, or pocket, and jot down the item and the price at the time of purchase. If you wait, you may forget something. Don't omit any purchase. If you buy a pack of chewing gum or a bag of potato chips, WRITE IT DOWN. Try to limit the amount of money that you spend on things you "want" and focus on spending money on things that you "need". Learn how to maximize your money. Don't purchase items that you know you can't afford. Before you make a high-priced purchase, figure out how you are going to balance your spending. For example, if you buy a pair of sneakers that cost $50 more than the average sneakers, then you will need to take $50 out of another "want" category. This means that you may not be able to buy the sneakers *and* the new video game or the new outfit. Regardless of the "want", you should never compromise your savings plan.

LESSON LEARNED: Think of a time you wasted money on something and then needed the money for something more important. How did you feel? Why do you think that it is important to get in the habit of saving money? Think about something you've wanted to buy but haven't bought because you don't have enough money. What are some things that you can do to earn the money that you need? How long would it take you to save up enough money to purchase what you want? Is it worth it to you?

Opportunity is missed by most people because it is dressed in overalls and looks like work.

— Thomas A. Edison

Chapter 11

Basic Training

There are a few essentials that you'll need to work on to make the transition from the Inner City to mainstream society. I am not suggesting that you lose your identity in order to fit into the main stream. However, you'll have to learn to be adaptable to the environment in which you find yourself. I know that this can be quite a challenge for young people who are growing up in the Inner City because that community has it's own culture. A lot of youth find it difficult to understand why they have to reflect a different image in mainstream communities, and they decide that they are going to be true to themselves. They feel that, if they have to change anything about themselves, then they are being phony or selling out. These same youth do not see anything wrong with changing fashion, language, and ideals based on what is "in" at the time.

I've seen urban youth who refuse to wear certain name brand expensive clothing because—according to "the word on the street"—that particular brand has played out. It doesn't matter if you have an entire wardrobe of that particular brand of clothing; you probably will never wear any of it again.

In the Inner City, young people tend to equate price with quality. The problem is, they will purchase expensive designer clothing but can't imagine saving for college. Many parents will give the youth money to purchase the most expensive outfits for the start of the school year but have a hard time understanding why they should purchase a life insurance policy. Some youth will spend their last money on an outfit knowing there isn't anything of substance to eat in their refrigerator. You see, in the Inner City sub-culture, appearance is important and, as a result, many young people will spend beyond their means just to look the part. When you stop to think about it, you're really being something that you're not. So, being willing to change to fit into mainstream society isn't all that different...certainly not as bad as some people make it seem.

I remember when the word "phat" made it's way into the urban sub-culture. I heard a few people use the word and thought it was sort of silly. But then again, so were "hype" and "def". Nonetheless, after awhile the words grew on me. They made sense. I used them regularly to describe something that was really nice, as everybody in the Inner City seemed to be able to relate to the lingo. But once the word "phat" made its debut, it was no longer cool to say that anything was "hype". Therefore, I stopped using that word. It wasn't long before the term "phat" had taken a back seat to "off the chain". So, if you think about it, you really aren't selling out on anything by changing to fit your environment. Survival and progression both require versatility. Don't ever confuse "versatility" with "selling out".

Mainstream society has a code and culture of its own. Two of the greatest contrasts between the Inner City and mainstream communities are the language and the dress codes. Although urban wear has become extremely popular in the main stream, there are still certain stereotypes, assumptions and stigmas attached to those who wear the clothes. I'm sure that this angers people who live in the Inner City, but let's take a look at it from a different perspective: If you were to see a strange white man dressed in a suit in the projects, what assumption would you make? Do you immediately assume that he's there on business—or to buy drugs? Would most delinquents clear out for fear that he is a detective or police officer? Much the same, you too will stick out like a sore thumb in mainstream communities in some urban wear.

Don't get it twisted. I am not suggesting that urban wear is bad, nor am I saying that you shouldn't wear it outside of the Inner City. What I am saying is that you should expect some people might prejudge you based on what you wear. If you are trying to fit into mainstream society for a particular reason such as employment, you'll have to decide if your principles are worth your missing an opportunity.

Young men, there's nothing wrong with your fashionable oversized gear and jewelry. And if you're into wearing your jeans below your waist, that too is your prerogative. Just understand that there is nothing original about your look. You fit in with almost any adolescent in the Inner City. I'm not condoning it, but you have to understand that there are some pre-conceived notions that mainstream society has attached to inner city youth who project a certain image. I've seen it result in innocent young men being harassed by the police and, in some cases, arrested. Now, if an occasional arrest is a consequence that you can live with, by all means, do what you feel is real. Otherwise, it might be in your best interest to incorporate some originality into your style. Your new look can still be urban, but you don't have to fit every police description.

Young ladies, if you're into wearing small midriff tees, and low riding tight jeans or shorts, it'll be difficult for me to tell you anything that can make you change. I can accept that, because change starts with the individual. I can only tell you that, in both the Inner City and the mainstream communities, that particular image is not one that is looked at with respect. Young men may lust after you, but that's not the image they would want for someone about whom they really care. If they saw their mother, sister, or even their steady girlfriend dressed in the same attire, they would probably be embarrassed or make a negative comment. Tight-fitting jeans may make you feel attractive, but whom are you attracting? Is this the image that you really want to project? You don't have to look ten years older than you are and expose your body to be beautiful. There's a way to be fashionable without compromising who you really are on the inside.

There's a time and a place for everything, and you've got to know what to wear to make the right impression. It only takes a few seconds for someone to form an opinion about you based on your appearance. It may seem like a small thing, but image makes a big difference. Think about it.

In mainstream America, the language of choice is English. The language that is understood is English, and the language that is accepted is English. Be prepared to use Standard English whenever necessary. This does not mean that the use of slang or Ebonics should be banned. This language is a part of the urban culture and is appropriate in many situations. The use of slang and Ebonics only becomes problematic when the user has not mastered the English language and is unable to understand when it is necessary to make the switch from Ebonics to English and vice-versa. You see, in the Inner City it's okay to walk up to a friend and say "What's good?" An expected response might be "I'm aight...chillin'". But in mainstream society, it's more appropriate to ask a stranger "How are you doing?" and an expected reply would be "I'm fine, thank you". I don't see anything wrong with using slang words and phrases, but first master the English language.

Non-verbal communication is just as important as verbal communication. You've got to work on mastering them both. In the Inner City we tend to be rather cautious when it comes to interacting with strangers. I think this is a pretty good rule. However, it doesn't mean that we shouldn't be able to smile or loosen up in the presence of strangers. We should be aware of our surroundings but approachable. It's all right to say "hello" to someone you don't know. It's also okay to smile if you happen to make eye contact with someone you don't know. Good interpersonal skills or the ability to effectively interact with others is a priceless attribute to possess. A good first impression can get your foot in many doors in both mainstream and inner city neighborhoods. But once you're in, you better be able to communicate effectively!

Lesson Learned: Think about a time when you (or someone you know) was judged by someone else based on outward appearance (what you were wearing). How did that make you feel? Think about a time when you formed an impression about someone based on how they looked and later found out you were wrong. Some examples might be calling someone a "nerd" because they didn't choose to dress in popular clothing or follow the latest fashion trends, or assuming that someone has short hair because they wear extensions or weave their hair. Why is it critical for you to understand the importance of using appropriate language and making suitable clothing choices?

Destiny is not a matter of chance,

it is a matter of choice;

it is not a thing to be waited for,

it is a thing to be achieved.

— William Jennings Bryan

CHAPTER 12

SHARING
THE DREAM

It may seem like you'll never figure things out. You may still be troubled by the idea of a "career choice". I mean, how can you take all of the things you're good at and narrow them down to one career? You may still be having difficulty figuring out what it is that you're good at. Don't worry; there are millions of adults who *still* haven't figured it out. You're "a work in progress". You're learning more and more about yourself each day. You'll continue to grow and change based on your experiences and how you handle them. Think of yourself as a kaleidoscope. With each turn you make, you'll be a little different...but always beautiful. Your life is made up of many pieces that come together to create the real "you".

I'll let you in on a little secret: I still haven't narrowed down my purpose in life. I know what I'm good at. I know what other people think that I'm good at. I know what I like doing, and I know what I hate to do. The problem is, when I pull all of that information together, I come up with several things I'd love to do. Nonetheless, there are some things about me that don't seem to change. First of all, I have always wanted to leave my mark on the world; I've always believed that I could do great things. Next, I get bored easily, so I don't usually like work that doesn't allow me to be creative. Most importantly, I have a strong desire to help others (especially the disadvantaged).

Since I was having trouble figuring it all out, I decided to work on several projects and goals to see which one felt right. The problem was, after awhile I always felt like I was wasting time. I felt this sense of urgency to figure things out. I felt like there was something I should be doing that would give me the feeling of completeness. I just couldn't seem to find the answer.

One night I had a dream. I dreamed that I had written a book and I was holding the manuscript and talking about the book with a friend. In the dream the friend asked the title of the book, and I told her, "Learning To Dream With Your Eyes Open". After that, I woke up. To my disappointment, I was in my bed and I hadn't written anything!! I sat up in bed, told my husband about the dream, and said that I was going to follow it. I decided to write a book that would help inner city youth. The dream helped me find a way to combine my passion for helping others improve their lives and my ability to write.

You see, even when you can't figure it all out, keep working towards your goals. It'll all come together in time. You are here to accomplish something special, and you don't get to leave until you do.

LESSON LEARNED: What do you think you were born to do? What steps do you plan to take in order to make sure you reach your goals? What is the one thing that makes you feel the most insecure about your plan or purpose? Why is it important for you to keep working towards achieving your goals even if you are uncertain? Also, I want you to familiarize yourself with the world outside of your community. Begin regularly reading the newspaper in its entirety (especially the international and business sections). If you have access to a computer, bookmark websites (such as msn.com.) that provide top stories and briefings.

Ego is acting like you're all-that.

Like they say on the block, "all-that."

Can't nobody touch you.

Confidence is knowing who you are.

— **Shaquille O'Neal**

CHAPTER 13

A QUIET CONFIDENCE

The end result of a successful journey will leave you feeling secure and confident. When you realize that you have the power to influence your destiny, you'll wonder how others can live and accept the societal limitations that have been predetermined for them. But be careful not to pre-judge; it happens to the best of us.

When you reach this plateau, you'll be able to add a new dynamic to mainstream society, and you'll be able to give something back to the Inner City. That is your responsibility. You've come to realize that success is not defined by material possessions. What you get is far less important than what you give back. You were born to make your mark on the world and to make the world a better place. You were born to lead, not to follow, and you'll reach the point where you are able to be an effective leader. Recognize that this was not the predetermined plan that was mapped out for you by some in mainstream society, but it was the predestined plan that was mapped out for you before you were even born. There are those who are expecting you to fail. Prove them wrong! There are those that are counting on you to succeed. Make them proud!

When you are self-assured, you realize that, even if the world owes you something, there's no use sitting around and waiting for it. You understand that, no matter what you achieve, there will always be those who think they are better than you simply because they grew up in a more affluent neighborhood. You've learned to accept that, because you know who you are.

You may still be followed by security when you shop, and although it may frustrate you from time to time, you're self-assured and can handle this. You understand that mainstream society may not always embrace you with open arms, but you've earned your position by making good decisions.

When you're self-assured, you are ready for the new challenges you have to face in order to accomplish new goals and actualize new dreams. When you reach true self-assuredness, you are not ashamed of where you come from. On the contrary, you'll be able to speak loudly about your experiences in the Inner City. These are the experiences that influence who you are.

When you are self-confident, you're not afraid of where you're going; you understand that it doesn't matter where you go when you have mastered the art of versatility. You can converse with the best in the main stream and can still hold your own in "the hood".

When you've reached this point in your journey, you'll be discontented with mediocrity and operate on the principle that satisfaction is the result of knowing you've given your best. When your self-confidence has replaced your self-doubt, there'll be no need to make a public announcement. It will show in everything you do. It'll be a part of who you are. Your dreams will become your reality, and you will be fulfilled.

When you learn to dream, your passions become your canvas, and your actions are your paintbrush. When you learn to dream, you create your own masterpieces. Therefore, although you are grateful for each goal you reach, you know there are always new challenges to conquer and bigger dreams waiting to become your reality. So keep your eyes open wide, and dream on.

LESSON LEARNED: Spend a few minutes thinking about how you will feel when you have achieved your goals and made a successful life for yourself. Who do you think will be proud of your accomplishments? How do you think you will share your dream with the world? Do you think that you are ready to start dreaming with your eyes open? Are you inspired to make the most out of your life? Do you believe that you can be successful? Why is it important for you to have confidence in yourself? Take a moment to think about the following quote:

Right now you are one choice away from a new beginning—one that leads you toward becoming the fullest human being you can be.

— Oprah Winfrey

SUGGESTED READING

M.D., Carson, Ben and Murphey, Cecil. Gifted Hands: The Ben Carson Story. Zondervan, 1996.

Corwin, Miles. And Still We Rise: The Trials and Triumphs of Twelve Gifted Inner-City Students. Perennial, 2001.

Davis, Sampson, Jenkins, George, Hunt, Rameck and Draper, Sharon M. We Beat the Street: How a Friendship Led to Success. Dutton, 1st ed edition, 2005.

Dr. Davis, Sampson, Dr. Jenkins, George, Dr. Hunt, Rameck and Frazier, Lisa. The Pact: Three Young Men Make a Promise and Fulfill a Dream. Riverhead, Reissue edition, 2003

Gray, Farrah and Harris, Fran. Reallionaire: Nine Steps to Becoming Rich from the Inside Out. HCI, 2005

Jacob, Iris. <u>My Sisters' Voices: Teenage Girls of Color Speak Out</u>. Owl Books, 1st Owl edition, 2002.

Oldman, Mark, Hamadeh, Samer and Princeton Review. <u>The Internship Bible, 2004 edition (Princeton Review Series)</u>. Princeton Review, 2004 edition, 2004.

Russo, Joseph A. <u>Scholarship Handbook 2005: All-New 8th Edition College Board Scholarship Handbook</u>. College Board, 8th edition, 2004

Suskind, Ron. <u>A Hope in the Unseen: An American Odyssey from the Inner City to the Ivy League</u>. Broadway, reprint edition, 1999.

Vanzant, Iyanla. <u>Don't Give It Away! : A Workbook of Self-Awareness and Self-Affirmations for Young Women</u>. Fireside, 1999.

Has this book inspired you to pursue your dreams?

If so, the author wants to know about it!!!

Send your letters to:
Learning Series Press
Attn: Melanie Geddes
P.O. Box 590812
Fort Lauderdale, FL 33359

Or send an email to the author at:
mdgeddes@learningtodream.com

*Excerpts from some letters will be posted on the website!

ORDER FORM

For quantity orders (10+)
call Learning Series Press at (800) 714-0309

Single copies may be ordered from popular online bookstores
and from www.learningtodream.com
or you may use the order form below:

Name: _____

Company: _____

Mailing Address: _____

City & State: _____

Telephone: _____

Fax: _____

E-mail: _____

Please send ____ copy (copies) of Learning to Dream With
Your Eyes Open @$10.95 per copy.
(For books shipped to Florida addresses please add 6% sales tax)

Make Check/Money Order payable to:

Learning Series Press

Please charge my credit card.

Credit Card: ☐ Visa   ☐ MC   ☐ Amex

Card #: _____

Expiration Date: _____

Signature of Cardholder: _____

Please mail/fax/e-mail your order form to:

Learning Series Press
P.O. Box 590812
Fort Lauderdale, FL 33359
Fax: (305) 390-8724
E-mail: order@learningtodream.com

Please add $4 shipping and handling.

ORDER FORM

For quantity orders (10+)
call Learning Series Press at (800) 714-0309

Single copies may be ordered from popular online bookstores
and from www.learningtodream.com
or you may use the order form below:

Name: _____

Company: _____

Mailing Address: _____

City & State: _____

Telephone: _____

Fax: _____

E-mail: _____

Please send _____ copy (copies) of Learning to Dream With
Your Eyes Open @$10.95 per copy.
(For books shipped to Florida addresses please add 6% sales tax)

Make Check/Money Order payable to:

Learning Series Press

Please charge my credit card.

Credit Card: ☐ Visa ☐ MC ☐ Amex

Card #: _____

Expiration Date: _____

Signature of Cardholder: _____
Please mail/fax/e-mail your order form to:

Learning Series Press
P.O. Box 590812
Fort Lauderdale, FL 33359
Fax: (305) 390-8724
E-mail: order@learningtodream.com

Please add $4 shipping and handling.